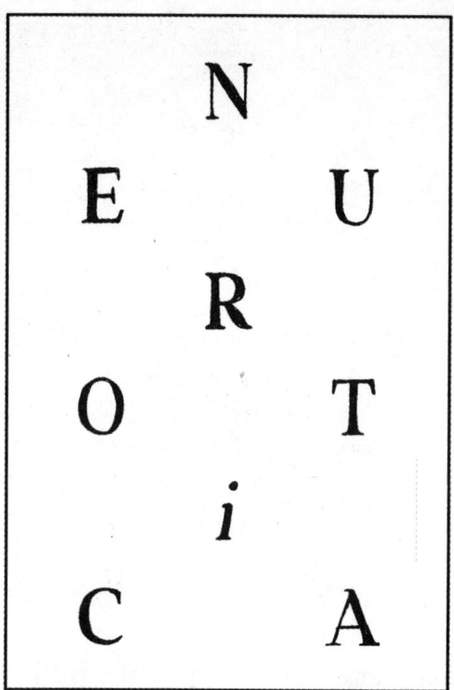

poems

MAXWELL I. GOLD

A SHORTWAVE BOOK

Text Copyright © 2026 by Maxwell I. Gold

All rights reserved. No part of this book may be reproduced in any form or by any electronic or mechanical means, including information storage and retrieval systems, and may not be used to train Large Language Models or Artificial Intelligence, without prior written permission from the publisher.

SHORTWAVE PUBLISHING
Publisher's full catalog available at:
shortwavepublishing.com

SIMON & SCHUSTER
Worldwide sales and distribution:
simonandschuster.biz

Publisher's Note: No generative Large Language Models or Artifical Intelligence were used during any part of the production of this book.

FIRST SHORTWAVE EDITION — APRIL 2026

COVER ART AND INTERIOR DESIGN
BY ALAN LASTUFKA

10 9 8 7 6 5 4 3 2 1

ISBN 979-8-897320-26-4 (Paperback)
ISBN 979-8-897320-27-1 (eBook)

CONTENTS

A Lexicon of Phosphorous and Memory: Max Gold's *Neurotica*

1. Here are a few words about poetry (paraphrased):

2. Emily Dickinson: I know it is poetry if it takes off the top of my head.

3. Robert Frost: poetry is what gets lost in translation.

4. Robert Penn Warren: poetry is about the creation of the self.

5. Percy Shelley: poets are the unacknowledged legislators of the world.

6. One more? That bit from Wordsworth and Coleridge about poetry being the spontaneous overflow of emotion recollected in a moment of tranquility. (As I understand it, Coleridge thought this was only a partial description of poetry, which a survey of his most famous work would support. But let's leave that alone.)

7. These are the quotations that come to my mind when I think about poetry. There are more (Archibald MacLeish's "A poem should not mean / But be") but that isn't the point.

What is, is that these words function for me as signposts, as a means to orient myself within whatever textual landscape I'm traversing. Although I'm a big fan of formal poetry (meter, rhyme, all that stuff), there isn't anything about the necessity of those elements to make poetry, poetry. I suppose you could find a little of that in the Wordsworth-Coleridge quotation, but the requirements they specify have to do with the emotional states necessary for the inspiration and then composition of a poem. Instead, the words of these signposts chart the ways in which a reader recognizes and responds to poetry, both in terms of its effect upon them and its exploitation of the characteristics of the language in which it's written (Dickinson and Frost, respectively). They offer a way to think about how a poet's body of work, collected in a single volume or taken as a whole, contributes to the formation of something greater than the individual work, to a kind of overarching sensibility that turns the poet's name into an adjective, i.e. Shakespearean (this from Warren). They make hyperbolic claims about the power of poetry—though given how upset those in power can be made by it, there is probably something to the exaggeration (this from Shelley). And they remind me of the importance of reflection both in the composition of poetry and (I would argue) in its reading (Wordsworth and Coleridge).

8. Which brings me to Max Gold's excellent book of poems. In reading (and re-reading) *Neurotica*, the quotation/signpost I find myself using as a guide is Warren's concerning the construction of the self. From "In the Beginning, I was Afraid" to "Towards the End, I Was Broken," with stops along the way for such poems as "Hebrew School Dreams," "A Prelude to Madness," and "Farewell to Earth (Words No More),"

we watch a self being built, assembled from shards of memory and dream, text and image. It's hard not to be reminded of T.S. Eliot's line at the closing of *The Waste Land* about shoring up fragments against his ruin. Max Gold's work is similarly far-reaching and eclectic in its bricolage. But there's a directness in these poems, a willingness to meet experience frankly, in all its complexity and messiness, that marks them as the product of a post-Confessional sensibility, one willing to engage straightforwardly with its conflicts and contradictions. In their tendency toward baroque and grotesque imagery to explore the precincts of the self, these poems echo Baudelaire, but a Baudelaire familiar with the tropes and imagery of weird and horror fiction. The end of *The Waste Land* evokes a medieval structure, a keep in a state of collapse, its walls propped up by loose timber and slabs of rock. The poems in *Neurotica* evoke a more contemporary ruin, a thing of crumbling concrete and glass, studded with mirrors, surrounded by pitted and pockmarked highways.

9. Another signpost I've found useful: the Wordsworth and Coleridge one about the spontaneous overflow of emotion recollected in a moment of tranquility. It's in these instances of (relative) calm that a poet finds the technique best suited to the emotion they're trying to re-collect. In the case of the poems in *Neurotica*, the techniques include anaphora, the use of the same or similar words or phrases to begin successive lines of verse. (Think Walt Whitman.) Returning the poem to a single word or phrase has an incantatory effect, rendering it almost a shamanic utterance. At the same time, its obsessive repetition makes anaphora particularly well-suited for representing the experience of neurotic thoughts. Shamanistic neurosis? Sure.

10. Is Max Gold one of the unacknowledged legislators of the world? Yes, he rules.

11. Is *Neurotica* poetry? Witness my skull, blown open, the contents still steaming.

– John Langan

N

E U

R

O T

i

C A

I. A Useless Yesterday

Neurotic is

Useless and functional,
    articulate madness
Singing the same songs
    that never seem to
Make sense despite the melodies
    Being easy to so easy to remember,
Useless and functional.

In the Beginning, I Was Afraid

Long since the first words
left my tired lips,
doubt filled my tired body
hungry with rage and discontent
the placations soothing for now,
some tenebrific beast herding
my insides and their defeated, blood-beaten flesh-castles
to the last point of a deep, pleasurable rupture
whereupon I fell towards the blackest,
most desolate emptiness
too tired since the first words
left my lips—
I was afraid

The Empty

Here, there was nothing—
Perhaps a twinkling dawn, or sign of decay
Only faint scratch marks on the walls of my skull
Left there to rot or as remembrance that everything
    decays, eventually—that nothing grows in the Empty
    beneath the pitch dark, twisted veils where unborn
    stars ne'er burn the beyond iron gates of someday.
Here, there was nothing.

Locō (from a Place)

Indifferent were the movements
where I went, what I did,
holding me to the ground;
without reason,
as long as I remained,
without movement,
I was safe, I was *told*;

Indifferent to the motions of the Earth
where it swayed, how my body reacted
held to the ground
without reason, or consent
as long as I *could move*,
I was safe, I was told;

Without indifference,
where I went, it didn't matter
holding me to the ground,
from one place to another
without reason,
as long as I remained,
I wasn't safe, anymore.

The Motions

i.

Going through the motions, evading the treacherous
    days,
felt as if I was lost in the havoc
of a psychopomp who danced to the corporate music,
wild and without the grace of motion
atop my fragile and weak body.

Going through the motions in a system that locked me,
and those who—acted like,
sounded like, even thought like me—
in metal boxes and far off closets.
The locks never opened,
only too late for the blissful masses
to find our corpses
shriveled up into some white, salient expendable plastic,
    smeared along the city streets
where broken hearts mixed with bemused cries, and
    deranged, toxic sacs of gray matter.

Would the locks be broken, I screamed.
Inside my head of course, for no one heard me
—heard us—going through the motions
in each box, chained down to the darkest ends;

ii.

Going through the motions like I'd been here before in
another system, another day, falling deeper, faster,
towards the bottom of the box,
going through the motions day by day without
constructs, or the light of reasons, and the inability to
evade the treachery of days
going through the fucking motions when I thought I'd
lose my mind and forget myself, unless I conformed
to *their* ways; affirmed beliefs which destroyed my
own if it meant,
Going through the motions, again and again and maybe
they'd let me out of the box.

Going through the motions was a vomitous curse,
sloshed in the pits of convention, I waited, unable to
force the hatch open.

A Stretch of Highway

Alone at night, drifting
    through the fog and funk
        of misguided expectations
        beneath illuminated concrete
        pathways
        where
        ivory
        pillars
    like ghosts climbed
    into the skies
haunting my peripheries'
    begged me to glide
        faster
        and
        faster,
        without control
        without reason,
until I smashed into some
        unknown oblivion;
Faster without any hope I thought I'd escape driving
    away
from myself—a piece of night, cracked and old
reflected the world I never wanted—
    that never wanted me, parts of me,

side to side, losing parts of myself
along the gravel path
too afraid to glare back
into the refracted nothingness where
objects in the rearview mirrors
appeared closer than they ought to be
and roadmaps were useless
surrounded
by phantoms who cried,
behind you, turn around!
Turn around,
quick,
though this was a one-way,
one stop illusion of choice alone at night
drifting through the darkest parts of myself
until all at once the smell of burnt rubber clotted my
nostrils when I realized the monsters were
everywhere.

Hebrew School Dreams

Gone inside those old Temples,
beneath stucco ceilings and plaster faces,
I wandered through both
familiar and strange places
where stained glass eyes glared
from five thousand years
the unquestionable elders
whose fingers painted green chalkboards,
pushed me into cheap wooden desks,
into the crowds of names
in hopes I'd find myself
in the shadow and song,
my doubts soon assimilated
by
expectations held hostage at the
crossroads of intersectionality
unsure if the closets I built
for myself were
safe enough,
Jewish enough,
queer enough
after the shattered signifiers
like bloody pieces of glass at my feet
still the scars lingered
despite any reclamations
I'd always remain trapped
between two worlds,

never quite malleable
within the stucco Temples
too cream-colored
for the rainbows
painting the stars above me,
always a fleck within the hazy murk
I clung to the possibilities
lurking someday
where that quiet, nerdy boy
played in the ruins of the past
with the imagination he never quite understood
before being brought to the Temple
realizing one day,
he'd finally be, enough

Yellow File Folder

File under dreams so demented, and carried inside the
altered yellow folder concealed my worst nightmares
and brightest hopes; scribbled and anxiously inked
onto wrinkled notebook paper as sacred as the most
ancient dogmatic bibles, no one understood them,
but treasured them just the same and were on the
flip-side ready to mock my constructed faith; stories
I wrote for myself, characters and places built in a
fragile consciousness hidden away in that yellow file;

The awkward, immutable silences covered in darkness
which curdled beneath old fingers clutched against
those wilted pages, praying no one would see or
touch to peel back my deepest truths, the stained
edges of myself, wrapped in naïve fantasy and the
bloated optimism of a closeted queer-boy who
dreamed beyond the realms of steel, plastic, and
concrete playgrounds into the whispered hopes, fears
where crumbled stucco Temples might be nothing
but ruins in the light of a Someday drawn as wild,
beautiful illustrations never mocked, bullied, or
locked away again—

I'd carry this tattered piece of myself with me forever as if the tethered-ball bruises along my brain scarred into the nightmares forever passed down through subconscious what-ifs and the haunts of *you'll never be good enough* over and over again, still, I'd carry this folder, file under dreams, no longer demented or estranged but clutched tighter until the papers were ripped apart like ashes sprinkled across the land only to be reborn in imagination and light and file under dreams, free of this yellow file folder.

My Grandfather, Winnie the Pooh

Oh! Storyteller, who walked with me
to the edge of a fabled wood
and cradled my imagination,
carrying it towards a place
filled with ancient trunks,
whimsical songs,
lungwort, spiderwort, and mushroomed towers,
whose promised conclusions
built my dreams where I
became the founder and king
of what-if and someday

Oh! Storyteller, with steps
like shadows, silent and desperate
crisscrossed o'er the oaken floors
of the deadwood,
pulled me deeper,
renewed by old fables
and inspired by new stories
new comforts,
and new dangers
like eyes peering through the thorny brush
prepared to take the best parts of me
swallowed and lost in the woods
chewed by all manner of beast and bear,
the possibilities unattainable

Oh! Storyteller though, he found me,
my storyteller,
my light,
constrained by the sinister
barbed vines
at the bottom of the path
in the deepest parts of the world.

Oh! Storyteller, whose words,
while dipped in the stench of the phantastic
—they were the only words I knew—
the last promises given to me,
carried forever now in silk,
dreams and sorrow,
and the whimsy of a bear.

A Prelude to Madness

i. The Music Nobody Hears

When all was silent and awful,
those were the most
wonderful moments

in my life. Unable to see
through the haze
and clear the static

within my thoughts,
I found solemnity
within loneliness

so sweet. When the world
was cruel, loud, bright
and unforgiving

those were the most
terrifying sounds
I'd ever known—and still—

the most wonderful moments
were found within the music
that nobody ever hears,
except me when all was silent and cold.

ii. Expose

There was a place in the
middle of my thoughts far from
Doubt though I found
myself trapped
always
coming back
to the middle of nowhere
like the anxious, relentless storms
which kept me awake whose
winds ripped my scar-tissue and
memory
away
leaving only

vague dreams, and
splattered bits of consciousness across
that pink and panicked organ
my gem-guttered
homage to a useless, empty
temple of self-destruction,
whose phallic gods
screamed fantasy and fuckery
toward oblivion,
pragmatic obfuscation,
me in the middle of my thoughts
coming back
to a place covered in ruins

Doubt, like a shadow
covered everything
myself confined
always
leaving only

vague dreams
in the middle of my thoughts
this place called Nowhere
take me
away
exile me
through flame and reason
until nothing was left except
floating bits of a sad exegesis
nameless, boneless, and bereft
lost a dark revelation
leaving only
myself
always
coming back
to this place called
Nowhere

iii. I Wonder

When the lights stop flickering
and the stars go out,
I wonder
what might fill the emptiness
above me and I find solace
in the new graveyards
where no music can be heard;

When my hands cease
their wretched convulsing
and my brain no longer seized
in my tired soul,
I wonder
what will be left behind,
if anything for me,
or in the ruins of an old world
I wonder
in desperation at the curse of indecision;

When my voice cracks
with a last pitiful cloud of dust and blood,
and I stand at the rusted Gates of Nowhere
whose crooked arches bend
towards an unknown tomorrow,
I wonder
what pieces of me
were worth keeping or
who kept them,
who remembered them,

and I wonder if it was all worth it.

Walks Alone at Night

Steps into the cold, lonely dark,
    along broken concrete memories
I watched what was left of me
    dwindle into something unknowable—

down a winding road
    where I hoped I might
find the shred of something familiar,
    something that used to belong to me;
dignity like diamonds sparkling
    through the fog collecting beneath
footsteps of a ghost inside a fractured,
    soft-spoken someday where step by step
towards the frozen and endless night,
    I carried myself along scarred and scorched
pieces of estranged something-or-others.

The Longest Day

We need to talk, began a phone call, a moment
centralized deep within the cosmically wrenched
center of existence, a voice whose mundanity spoke
without cause or passion,

We need to talk—about the times how my soul felt so
easily replaceable, calculated, and manufactured
into a piece of something or other like cardboard,
computerized slate wiped clean from the memory of
those who I thought were everything and nothing
and still,

We need to talk o'er the dread-humdrums over coffee and
chaos with the night-capped bottles of raised clock
punches and mechanical arms drawn down over the
whistle-music, screaming, saluting,

We need to talk, to remind you, and me, that the days
were only days and never long enough that they
were fractured pieces of parts never meant to have to
ourselves until the clock ran dry,

We need to talk, came raspy voices through the walls in
my head, in my home, creeping from the safest places
that were anything but crooning tiny nightmares,

We need to talk, compressed harbingers said, in the
darkest part of myself prepared me for what would be
the longest day.

A Song for Me (I Lived)

I lived, and breathed fire whose smoke danced the
tantalizing dance of someday—maybe it was a dream
or hallucination
I lived or was it a lie, never expressed my own truth
I lived falsely in darkness and death, waiting for reality
that'd never come falling through a vault of stars
I lived without freedom, or anthems of Others—the
restrains from wasted days
I lived over and over until thrown out, thrown up into
the gutters and grime—reused, recycled for a body
that I never wanted
I lived as if a cipher, never understood by others or
myself buried deep in some sand-storm unable to
breathe; unable to think; unable to cry; unable to
sing; unable to die
I lived in a universe composed by self-made void-
vacuums, without air until my brain was all but
spaghetti inside my cracked skull, twisted into
something that it was never meant to be,
I lived a joke, the twinked-up punch line no-one
understood, glasses and gods too great for me to even
worship; for me
to beg; for me to escape the monster of
expectation; for me to walk the silver streets in
glittering cities; for me to
laugh at myself even if it was only to make the
world seem bearable for one moment; for me to
believe my own eyes,

I lived in nameless spaces that were never mine,
dungeons painted with my own insecurity where the walls grew ever
higher despite my intention to flee them; to fly away; to break away and sing; to finally look unto the endlessness that was the night;
I lived, embracing the music that held me close, cursing me in the words *everything's going to be all right*; cursing me
the world would change; cursing me to *moderate* or *modulate* myself, for *my sake*; cursing me
I lived, and breathed singing a song for myself, no matter if it was a dream; no matter if it was the end of days; no matter
if the stars fell in dread-bodies around me covering the world in flame; no matter if it meant painful drumbeats of war and wrath, I lived.

Inside a Corporate Dining Hall

I was surrounded by black suits,
spreadsheets spreading out, numbers,
and numbing sensations
painting the Art Deco gallery
of a crumbling, forgotten temple
I could barely breathe,
barely move, barely find myself
in the scent of plastic,
pressed thoughts which like those suits
would eventually wrinkle in time,
and crinkle into the flesh-fabric
of my heavy madness,
surrounded by black suits,
    forever

Fake smiles, corporate dreams,
only the rattled the chains,
dreams which were never mine,
but these awful ghosts;
too numerous to count as they
danced along the tiled prospects,
nimbly searching for tactical weakness
as if to strategize all possible futures
so that I might do better than them,
to avoid the dread-outcomes
they never understood, or worse,
never experienced,
asphyxiated by black suits,
    always

These were the ghosts of my history,
my regretful ancestors,
bemoaning the songs of what-if
inside crooked hallways
carved throughout my mind
while I stared into the
stone-faced suits,
uncaring,
indifferent;
soon-to-be ghosts themselves
they looked onward while we sat
in the cold, empty hall,
surrounded by black suits,
    never

Myself, another number,
another failed calculation of a boy
who failed to grow up,
cradled in the estranged arms of something
    misunderstood, surrounded by black suits and
    spreadsheets,
spreading out, endlessly,
and without a care in the world
surrounded by black suits
    infinitely and always

The Empty-ness

Here, I found myself again—find ourselves, again—
familiar and cold, no more dawn
or walls to scratch but the broken house of tomorrow,
an idea overrun by the vines and vice-grip twines
Too proud to loosen themselves
from my skull o'er the withered bleakness atop a
shattered piece of bone that used to be me.
Here, I found myself beyond nothing.

II. Tomorrows Colored in Apocalpyse

Neurotic is…

The End and the Beginning,
unexplainable and unreasonable,
a tomorrow colored
by wild visions
of a fetishized apocalypse;
The End and the Beginning.

Pogrom

Silent havoc, the promise of an indifferent tomorrow
rolled through modern cities with
Complacent eyes and carnivorous hearts
burned the bodies, swallowed the stars
leaving only the dark, dismal air
swallowed in smoke, mobs, and dread songs,
mobilized under silence worse than death,
whistled louder than the trains,
taller than the columns of ash and promises never-again,
wider than the tracks which snaked through cold towns,
dismembered peoples who were born,
no, raised with the false sense of security
until the anthems Flame, Metal, and Untruth,
The Brothers of Havoc smashed cities
and systems leaving us with nothing.

§175

Through bizarre temples built with parchment and
burnt words, codified by unreasonable nomenclature,
whose restrictive bailments kept us locked away,
colored and contextured by orientation and love;
here the paragraphs were taken down as if an unholy
commandment written by gods that were never ours.

The words themselves put down not in ink, but the
blood of so many like us, the Queen-Goddesses who
fell in the stone streets where the blue-bald thugs
laughed at their glitter and gold; the Yellow Stars and
Pink Lights who burned underneath the cigarette and
concentration of neon flames by the fires of progress.
All tenants wrought by words which were never
meant to, but still linger like the ghosts of yesterday.

The ruined Temple of Nomenclature, bodies of signifiers
spilling out of the Cosmic Bath Houses, scattered
across the stars not only for the world to see but
confined inside our closets where the fingers of new
corporate gods hoped to press us further, deeper; the
words of their awful prayers forever codified as if we
never-were or *never-could-be.*

Though, this was for the Queen Goddesses, Yellow
Stars, and Vogue-Mothers who damned the
commandments of an old world that never wanted
them in the first place, who cried in languages of
love,
rage,
and light;
to leave behind not ruins of a nameless temple, or
phrases that beg to categorize, conflate, and ascribe
meaningless affirmation to existence, but throw into
the pyres of Someday, the bodies of old, white gods
who never knew
the love,
rage,
and light;
to deconstruct the universe with their final cry,
Down
with
175!

When Trains Were Devils

The houses at the edge of my worst fears were worn like a soldier's helmet, huge and ugly, for the world to see. Compressed against my skull, the ability to move from one place to another felt like a fantasy. Even though I knew they were coming for us; coming for me. Gliding across the earth in metal boxes, freely, though a matter of perspectives, towards the end; without concern or presumed by ignorance that everything might be okay when we knew it wasn't.

Towards the old station with great metal walls, and wooden graveyards whose thorny eyes peered from the other side of an empty, hopeless railyard. The sounds of boots, blood, and baleful promises lingered in the mud and murk of the air when the door slid on their rusty hinges, voices sung from the gray clouds, but we never left the metal boxes. Never again, quaked my heart when the boots blundered the earth and ancient wheels wallowed in the misty death of concentrated motion.

The Trashman Cometh: A Most Well-Deserved Oblivion

i. The Rumbling

Beneath the oldest known spaces of a tired, humble earth
where grim specters moaned in ghastly shadows,
I bathed in the awful secrets of Tomorrow. Secrets
buried and thought they burned, stirred in the ash
and oak coffins whereupon old smiles waxed towards
a nameless hopeless, one forged in dread.

Precious nights, the last few which danced o'er the ruins
of a shattered star-covered palace whose high towers
bent towards blood-soaked spires, unable to keep
from quivering, stone and ash-like powder fallen
from ancient bodies as if warning me—us—not to
seek that which lies beyond the faceless throne at the
bottom of the world.

The rumbling cometh,
bit by bit
And the world watched,

Rumbling louder, below my feet, light and heat mixed
into something which pulled at my thoughts like
strings caught between my teeth, painfully sharp—
inextricably linked to those dark moments of
truth. Blood mixed with saliva and wild visions the
heartbeat of a haggard truth.

The rumbling cometh,
bit by bit
and the world watched,
and the world ignored me,
one by one,

as the old palaces crumbled around them, their ancient corpses piled higher in heaps of new and wild forms—The Future—while the ground ruptured violently.
Louder, deeper, the pit yawned revealing more to me than something visceral and bizarre beneath the oldest known spaces of a tired, humble earth;

The rumbling cometh,
bit by bit
and the world watched,
and the world ignored me,
one by one;

I saw the end, covered with more than fire, bone, and muck, but the inability and indecision of a people whose words became hollow, useless tools unable to combat the darkness, or perilous prophecies constructed by false-flesh. Too eager to comfort the mythology of a grim specter moaning in ghastly shadows, prepared to drown them in the awful secrets of Tomorrow.

I saw everything, and the rumbling cometh,
bit by bit
and the world watched,
Damn them!
One by one.

ii. Behold, the Pit

Pieces of the Future tumbled from the hopeless and
harrowed lips of faceless gods who lumbered
ceaselessly through the fog and haze of a starless sky.
Bits of tomorrow like ash and mold, or discarded
leftovers fell helplessly from that terrible beast.
Compressed beneath the boot and boned-up maniacs
who clamored at the feet of a monstrous inevitability,
laughing, singing its praises,

All Hail!
The Trashman cometh!

Skeletal bodies of what used to be people or possibly
something else swayed in the darkened, dismal
emptiness that replaced the skies, now full of
viridescent clouds. There, in the wake of a grotesque
and jagged cavity which appeared to cut ceaselessly
into the bosom of the world, swallowed any hope I
had for the Future.

Useless, chewed up like some flesh-toy, swallowed behind
salt-water-swords, I craned my neck higher towards
the immensity that was the Trashman, covered in
wiry pieces of shadow and light as if a colossus strode
forth from the darkest, most ancient stars. And yet,
wild sycophantic songs chorused around me as if to
greet the soulless harbinger, while the stars went out
all around me simultaneously pleading,

Someday told us,
Someday warned us,
The Trashman Cometh!

No more would I pity a world,
who begged for fire and falsehoods.

No more would I spare a kind word,
for those who embraced *Our Death*, and sought
repentance for
their doom;

No more would I wait,
in hopes the stars might burn with hope, but
welcomed our
despair.

iii. Oh! Despair

Everyone was gone,
inside a black and brutal existence
wrought by the awakening of the great, cosmic Waste-
God whereupon we became nothing
except immutable pieces of trash, flesh, light, and sound,
inside his cosmic slaughterhouse,
waiting for our turn to be re-used,
upcycled into something twisted,
something *other than*,
darker than what we'd ever imagined ourselves to be,
something deranged,
crumbling beneath the bleakest possibility,
multiplied infinity greater until the incomprehensible
and unknowable consequences pulled us,
ripped, and ruptured what was left of us,
and that was only the beginning,

and our blurred last moments,
captured chiefly through the stars
who sung towards seven planets now seven curses;
riddled with diseased choice like the bones of a man who
conquered everything, and was left with nothing,
blood replaced by oil and nightmares,
quickly extrapolated by the plastic, steel, and rhizomatic
what-ifs which covered a now broken world
—and the Trashman would soon come
to collect for us all,
that terrible ennobled innovator,

Someday told us,
Somebody warned us
All Hail!
The Trashman Cometh!

We: A Poem of Collapse

i

We stood at the end of the world
Together while stars fell,
wrapped in shrapnel and swords
whose blades cut down the promise of tomorrow

We stood in the rubble of Star and Moons
cosmic bodies twisted by crimson words,
conflated by lies and flaming eyes

We stood together on the precipice with backs turned
to the drumbeats of infinity
driving us towards blood-pits of rot,
ash, and hopeless nights

We carried onwards, in the face of reckless tumult,
nameless and cruel with sycophantic featly,
sworn to the fat, unsatisfied gods

We saw Star and Moon
caught betwixt cosmic gears of the Great Machine
unable to turn back the tides of destruction,

We pressed our bodies against the night
illuminated with songs of flame and death,
unable to climb towards the sky
through soot and sinewy murk,
until the final reprise

We sung a last refrain where
music held joy no longer
at the end of the world

We cried, both Star and Moon together,
felled like rotting trunks
into the black, sticky pits of never-again
We stood at the end of the world
Together

ii

We saw the wells run dry,
robbed completely or worth
No more water, oil, or blood
in the new world
Only dreams built on bodies
filled with
Cyanide and bile,
sentenced to oblivion

We were condemned forever
within ash and dirt
wandering through cities of torn apart
by false-history
Dried up, wasted,
and drunk on the mythology
Of what-used-to-be,

Blind

To what-never-could-be
in a broken dream whose skies were
painted with chemtrail-clouds, translucent-stars
glowing dimly in a spectral, collapsed pit
plastic giants risen from corporate grave-forges,
the boson-slaves of Crimson Faced warlords
who crafted this brave new world

We waded into our brave new nightmare,
inherited from ungrateful, Ivory Goblins
crooning like rusty squeeze boxes,
sad bedtime stories of old stars, blue planets
trapped in glass domes,
sucking in greenhouse fumes which filled our lungs

We prayed our world not be extinguished,
saved in form and memory
kept safe from them
until the putridness of reality,
the too-good-to be true-time-bomb blast mushroomed
with rapacious toxicity, burning what remained of the
old world's menageries leaving everything shattered,
never whole again
a piece of ourselves slammed into
the closets of memory, sealed away like a beast,

We were the children of the Future,
blamed and condemned to pick up the bones
in a broken, dried up place
stripped of its name
robbed completely of worth
at the end of the world
together while stars fell,
wrapped in shrapnel and swords
whose blades cut down the promise of tomorrow

How Impossible is 2045? (Nonsense from One Hundred Years Ago)

Everything was moving too fast,
far far away from the memories of dark days
one hundred years in the future,
one hundred bodies skewered
with bayonet and brand-name curses,
blasted across the darkest, remote woods of history—
roses once bloomed here,
on the shores of familiar coastlines,
suddenly ripped apart by brazen words—
too proud to listen
too cold to see
too empty to watch
while the winds ripped the earth,
loveless and barren,
swallowed thorn, brush,
and the brittleness of possibility.

Petals fallen to the ground,
dead-headed by silver blades
whose hungry glaives danced drunk and delirious,
blacked out by gravities' sweet, intoxicants
too powerful to keep us from swallowing ourselves
in tired and lazy entropy until
our days were saggy, fat, and tired,
bereft of something we knew of longing like a hand
upon the water—long shadows and wrinkled bodies
we used to know,
left to wither into something dark, strange,
and truly unmentionable—

none of it made any sense—
the nothingness of the everyday,
the pain of yesterday one hundred years ago
when the world moved without pallid anxiety,
without the fear it would stop tomorrow
like ballooned humdrums that weren't light enough
to carry us onward anymore
through the atomic weightlessness of
someday, what-if, and could-be—
tossed away like toy-corpses into
rusted trunks of yellow-cabs and taxi-maybe's,

I found that hallowed vestibule of the Everyman,
a hollow, amber shell,
tattered and ferried
along asphalt tributaries,
its rickety metal hull a slave to the masses
who demand its services,
objectified its utility without
concern or consequence
despite the desire for the pleasure it provided
One wheel after the other riding along the rocks,
begging—no—clamoring,
the pathetic yellow thing, sung its sad song,
The Song of the Everyman,
Over and over screaming into the night, ref
too proud to listen
too cold to see
too empty to watch,

the dark fate destined to find swallow the seas and stars
in the long-tired days of tomorrow
while the winds ripped the earth,
loveless and barren,
swallowed thorn, brush,
and the brittleness of possibility.

Still, everything moved too fast.

White roses, perfumes of the sea
lingered from the salt and sanctuary
whose song-strums broke barriers
where old lighthouses on familiar coastlines
trembled and teetered along rocky ridgelines,
their ancient bodies moaned,
how impossible is it?

One hundred years ago,
one hundred stones collected
before the sea swallowed the old world
And the lighthouse laughed,
how impossible is it?
One hundred years later,
one hundred stones drowned in salt and regret
beneath the folly of progress-plans
dim reminders of what-used-to-be,

a song of nonsense left for the future
whose music might never be heard
squawk and squeal,
bird and brackish beast loomed overhead,
feathers like roses glistened in the new sun
hotter, brighter,
more vengeful and unforgiving
while the stones and light-masters
leaned into the coastlines,
the music becoming something of a faint prayer,
The New Song of the Everyman,
    Everything moves too fast,
until it doesn't
one hundred years from the beginning of the end,
where I wondered, truly, *how impossible is 2045?*

Cosmic Dysmorphia

In the eyes of the universe, nothing mattered.
        It didn't matter.
    I didn't matter.
Abominations conflated with pale
    notions of beauty and reason,
scarred me like some ancient disappointment
    as if I was a piece of parchment
never cut exactly to the right specifications, incorrectly
    measured—
        It didn't matter.
    I didn't matter.
And still, cutting deeper and deeper
    until there was nothing left except shards of regret,
    floating inside a pitiful vacuum. Strands of myself,
    and others
that never fit but were expected to fall in place;

Piece by piece, every part of myself
    reflected through glass
bones, and smarmy silhouettes of what used to be,
    pallid cyber flakes flung
towards the periphery of old stars.
        It didn't matter.
    I didn't matter.

A towering uselessness,
    I saw the indifferent horizon
stretch wide and vast, soon cresting
    along the blackest edges of space
while I swelled in mass and mania; a smoldering piece of
    star-crusted emptiness. My anthem heard through
    the darkness, despite my false and twisted perceptions
    where in the
eyes of the universe nothing mattered except the ugly,
    unreasonable truth—
        It didn't matter,
            I didn't matter.

Beyond the Sterile Gate

Everyone was frozen, complacent like pieces of a zombified something or other in line to nowhere, waiting for something they might never see. A sterile future on the other side of a metallic gate, guarded by leather beasts and wicked prophecies; a push-card someday where no-questions-asked and silver smiles were enough while Crimson Faces loomed high over cybernetic temples. Timed feet and tender flesh carried themselves onward beneath the lidless gaze of a sinister tomorrow, sedated and sanguine without concern; the brain-soaked dreams derived by false-declarations until imagination was as wrinkled as the skin which it clung to.

The lines progressed slowly beyond rubber fingers and sterile placations towards a dark Elysium whose planes allowed nothing of majesty to its inhabitants. I had seen all this before as I dragged Yesterday's corpse through the Gate knowing Tomorrow might never come.

And So It Goes, The End That Cometh Sweetly

Every so often,
I miss the feeling of being alive.

The touch of someone's finger across my cheek, the blade
that strikes the hair on an ancient head, dull perfumes
and empty cabinets with knick-knacks collecting the
stale suggestions of what-if and maybe-so. So it goes
beneath a bunker of stars,
I cowered under blankets of withered dreams, the
famous last words of a dead man.

I miss them.
I miss the lights.

The stars, even the dreadfulness which cavorts amongst
the quiet thoughts and candor of friends, I can't
help but miss those awkward stares. The banal
wonderment in the eyes of enemies which crackles
like the last bitter embers of a candle.

I miss it,
but damn the lights.

So it goes, as the blood turns brown,
and the flesh dries up there's nothing I wouldn't give to
watch the sands turn to glass under the long, dim
shores of tomorrow where nothing matters save for
the decayed bones of old gods.

I cursed them.

Even the cosmic flash-death which boils atom and
age beneath its rancid blasphemies was a sweetness
compared to the curses, the flesh-tubes, and bodies
that comprised of me.

Yet, I miss it.
And curse it to the end, that cometh sweetly for
us all.

Farewell to Earth (Words No More)

When words were no longer enough to comprehend the
beauty and devastation and became the tears I shed,
less than salt of the earth, beneath the hot, scorching
rays of a red star;

When worms were empty, useless signifiers unable to
promote any meaning in the meaningless glass deserts
marred with oxidized towers that once were filled
with flesh ants and plastic bobbles;

When words were anything else but fanciful
traumatization blasted into the night like a gas that
polluted the air;

When words were transformed into tools for wars
without end where banners emblazoned with the
demons of the Other Side marched across fields of
bone and blood, left shadows and ghosts in the wake
of a nuclear fire;

When words held no breath, no music, unable to stay
the storms beyond the horizons whose terrible
lightning blinded even the fiercest of us with visions
of a Tomorrow, we wished might never arrive to see
such wild and furious wrath;

When words were unable to console the smallest wounds
without grace or dignity creeping further into the
lowest corners of a corroded house whose foundations
were unfixable;

When words were bereft of reasonable meaning, still,
we fought despite the futility of our actions; still, we
fought helplessly;

When words reached across generations like some
hapless fog, uncaring and murky—unable to discern
where the fires truly started or who had the first or
last word;

When words were no longer enough to really mean
anything or arrest the truth in our hearts, we looked
up and proclaimed
Farewell to Earth.

The Cycle of ME

i. The Wreck of Me

Endlessly bruised and brittle was the corpse once known to the world as me. Beached upon some forgotten shoreline where storms were wretched and unholy; my resumed demise lingered in the fantastic and chimeric ruin while subsumed in bloated grayness of submerged idealism, oxidized my creamy hull. Even the waters attempted to belabor by untimely passing from this plane while happy parasites gnawed at what remained of sail and scorned bones, floating atop the salt and briny stars.

A fat, empty vessel, I was drained entirely of the booty thought safely secured in the dark, nameless depths—raided by hungry bandits who, wrapped in plastic and chains, beat their chests, and plundered my decayed body. *Treasure for the new world*, they proclaimed, the waters soon bereft of pity pulled me away from the shoreline while I watched the stars twinkle in hushed twilight anthems. *Treasure for the new world*, I cried, piece by piece, consumed by the sea, a corpse once known to the world as *me*.

ii. The Mirror of Me

Reflections so cruel
Self-scrummed images forged
in the worst moments of something too dark to see, but
thick enough to drown beneath, yet
too far for me to
see the monstrous thing swelling up through the muck
and inside me, self-destructive instincts, too hungry
to contemplate the words—too ugly to see anything
past the wretchedness of self-interest, a great thing
seething with muck and megalithic cruelty, still
trapped behind high walls and spikes; my self-
internalized fortresses too high to climb, too tall to
batter down, but sinister and ancient enough to wait;
waiting for me to let my guard down and break free;
toxic images of myself spewing from the decayed
innards of corroded consciousness, *let me out!* And I
ignored the final cries when in the worst moments,
too far for me to see the monstrous thing,
I knew I couldn't let *him* out, self-preservation battered
my soul like low trumpets in the bleak autumn
morning calling me, *let me out*, the anxious,
unrelenting cruelties welling up within ourselves like
an ostinato of strings gaining momentum, building
towards that chimeric end! Yes! A song which called
throughout the night, *we sang the collapse of me.*
Collapsed, tired, and complete, I sung the final words
in the worst moment,
in the face of that monstrous thing,
the collapse of me.

iii. Farewell to Me: Forms and Fuckery

A towering monster
wrapped in toxic expectations,
looming incredibly
like a mass of not-good-enoughs
and sinewed-suck-it-ups with wiry veins
across a heaving flesh-obelisk
wailed beautiful condemnations;
chorused by the putrescent moaning
of a billion sheeps in the night,
slowly dissipating in the face of a reckless dawn.

A monster awoken from
the worst parts of my tired
and twisted body,
believed to dwell inside me once,
the creature wrenched
from my belief and bone
thought too soon, to be exorcized
by deranged gym-room rituals
and jock-god chants
until the fear of what-if
and never-good-enough grew too powerful.

Swollen with grotesque numbness,
I was pushed back
through the aperture of my mind,
the closet door latched and shut,
I was a monster in name only
concealed from the world,
and a wreck no more,
but swallowed in death.

A Picture of Dead Stars in the Sky

When the last stars flicker no more, unable to whisper
fire or fantasy through the dark, I begged for
everything to end. And so too, when the last embers
of reason and empathy were replaced by wicked
and treasonous apathy, I recalled the picturesque,
glass-stained sky waning towards a blithe oblivion
whereupon I too might find rest.

Lingering beneath the heaviness of a cursed decision
there might not be stars to gaze upon when shadows
consumed my bleak reality. Shattered, *no wait*,
scattered across a wretched horizon I watched as the
last pitiful lights flickered in and out like my lungs
unable to contract a meager breath. In and out,
until I was unable to whisper fire or fantasy through
the thick, dark night when all that remained was a
picture of dead stars in the sky.

A Poem for the Apocalypse

Theories, divisions, and crooked words like scratched
up anthems sounded in the deep as if to warn us,
to warn me: something is coming. A call from the
gut gurgled by unconscious, depraved paranoia like
loudspeakers blaring across desensitized eardrums
coated in dried blood and sycophantic songs;
screamed 'everything will be over soon!'

Mindless, drool-dragon-stooges stomped their hooves on
marble dungeon floors, ignorant of velvet chains, and
white bone-bleached confetti as it rained from the
pixilated skies where ivory task masters cackled with
whips and wanton hatred, praising the destruction of
the Old Cities.

Soon, the iron gates came tumbling down, not by
force or by way of barbarous invaders, but willful
machinations as the Crimson Faces made their
triumphant parade with cyber-songs that wrenched
both reason and madness whereupon a mass of
zombified flesh that once were people droned
together *everything will be over soon*, as the sun and
stars fell behind the horizon in hideous, woeful
synchronization.

Structural Integrity (A List)

Our life
is
an inconvenience,
mine is
mindless,
unable to concentrate,
To negotiate a place
in a space
without navigating mundane
corridors inside my brain,
buried and constricted
in a fleshy ground cover
like a bizarre flesh jungle,
too far gone,
too messy to untangle
to see what horror
lies beneath and
find a way out
of the labyrinth that is me,
while I've inconvenienced too many,
with the imposter
who pressed me farther
underneath a space,
a nameless place,
a Nowhere I thought I'd conquered
but whose forces usurped my mind,
I thought was *mine*
but was never *mine*
and was only an inconvenience.

A Song for Trains

Help is on the way, across the old
tracks, might and grand
rumbled the metal beast
Help is on the way, through blight and barren
dreams the whistle cut the night down
until no stars flicked, shadows damned
Help is on the way and the people,
rejoiced, unaware while
iron fingers coiled tightly in rust and wrath
Help is on the way, across the old,
broken world

    cried the mothers,
        screamed the children
    beseeched the Light
    cackled the Liars,

Help is on the way beneath blood and baleful
lips,
    crimson devils
        who thought their machinations
clever and secret, snickered,
Help is on the way, across the old world.

Wash It Clean: To Wander or Die

To stay my feet, to remain chained would be the worst
of all possible crimes, subdued, confined to a space
whereupon I'd ne'er to wander or dream but in the
dust of a platitudinous someday. The nefarious forces
which dared to keep me tethered to a witless and
wistful existence acted on some dark ambition, but
I couldn't help myself—brought back by the urge to
run, to flee betwixt a wild and wondrous desolation
whose beautiful, spectral starstruck columns climbed
effortlessly towards a nameless heaven; I collapsed in
blithe joy at the sight, at the music which drew me
closer even by threat of death at the edge of Oblivion
who sought my ruin when the sun retreated beyond a
high peak, but still, those chains remained the worst
possible fate.

To stay, or to die in the presence of something so
terrible—a world without the ability to see what lurks
behind the old mountains or feel myself asphyxiated
by the thick and terrible indecision like chains around
my ankles. *No! I won't* I cried while the purpled night
spilled from beyond the rocky crags and the stars
in their mystic vaults who begged me not to stay
my feet, to remain chained, but embrace the wild
wanderlust that welled deep in my soul; or suffer that
which could be the worst of all possible fates.

Impractical Demons

I had destroyed that which mattered most, a body
composed with flesh and calcified dreams, now
pressed into some casket-closet until there was
nothing but a frail husk. My body taken for granted
until the pieces of something I thought were mine
taken away,
so willingly,
so easily, I didn't remember,

falling into the darkest pits, in the hands of impractical
monsters.

They pulled me farther, towards a heinous and ugly
something or other where nothing made sense—
nothing about this makes sense except for the
impractical demons perched on either shoulder
pounding on either side of my skull begging me
to make a decision, laughing while my brain bled,
unable to comprehend the collapse of the world
inside and out.

My world, I thought I understood, soon destroyed
through impractical demons and impractical
decisions

so willingly,
so easily, I didn't remember,

falling into the darkest pits, in the hands of impractical
monsters trapped in some casket-closet.

Neurotica

Neurotic is. . . useless and functional,
    articulate madness
Singing the same songs
    that never seem to
Make sense despite the melodies
    Being easy so to remember,
Useless and functional.

Ghosts from my youth
    And strange dreams
The take me back
    To places I've never
Wanted to see again, and
    Gods that stalk my nightmares.

Neurotic is, the End and the Beginning,
    unexplainable and unreasonable,
    a tomorrow colored
    by wild visions
    of a fetishized apocalypse;
The End and the Beginning.

Neurotic is the part of me
    that never made sense
    to show the world, but somehow
    found a way out of the
    constructs and closets,
    the corridors of doubt and
    derisive otherness that never made sense;

Neurotic is everything I never wanted
 and needed combined
 in a chemical bath of unreasonable questions
 smashed along the side of a stainless steel tub—
 one after the other—
 folded and flipped like some piece of dough,
 all the questions without answers I had to know,
 I had to ask and never wanted;

Neurotic is explosive and beautiful,
 a mushroomed cloud rising higher
 towards the ceiling of my brain
 until flesh like ash covered a bloody floor
 where there were no more
 questions or answers to be found,
 though the ghost of my consciousness
 wandering through a graveyard in my skull begged
 relentlessly for truth
 —or lies—
 or a piece of something
 in the aftermath of my incessant exploration
 that was too much for me to handle;

And neurotic is too much to handle
 while happily embraced
 as I find myself pulled across a thousand different roads
 which lead away from the ruins of me, all circling back
 to that place, *Nowhere*, *Someday*, and *Everyplace*;
Neurotic is everything, and nothing.

Towards the End, I Was Broken

A familiar journey,
and ancient songs
I saw what used to be landmarks
of a City of Skulls,
monuments erected for the terrible and awesome
visions which ruptured my brain,
over and over since I uttered those first words,
too long to remember
but their music continued to jilt me—
this reprise where fallen flesh-castles
now shriveled scar-lakes
towards the end,
I was broken

Reprints

§175, *Unspeakable Horrors 3: Dark Rainbows Rising*,
Crystal Lake Publishing

And So It Goes The End That Cometh Sweetly,
Shadows Over Mainstreet Volume 3, Bleeding Edge Books

All other titles are new for this collection.

About the Author

Maxwell I. Gold is a multiple award nominated author who writes prose poetry and short stories in weird and cosmic fiction. His work has appeared in numerous anthologies and magazines. Maxwell's books include the Bram Stoker Award nominated poetry collection *Bleeding Rainbows and Other Broken Spectrums*. He lives in Ohio with his husband and two dogs Marshall and Otto, and currently serves as the Executive Director for the Horror Writers Association.

Also by Maxwell I. Gold

Tiny Oblivions and Mutual Self Destructions

Bleeding Rainbows and Other Broken Spectrums

Oblivion in Flux

anOther Mythology

Thanks for reading!

For more Shortwave titles, visit us online. . .

OUR WEBSITE
shortwavepublishing.com

SOCIAL MEDIA
@shortwavebooks

EMAIL US
contact@shortwavepublishing.com